Preface

    There are three main reasons why I decided to put a few of my ideas, opinions, observations, and philosophies together and create this very small book.

    I strongly believe we all have something to contribute and I have ideas that I want to share. This is an attempt to share mine without the thousands of unnecessary words used in most books in order to fill a word count. I hope by sharing the wisdom I have gained from my own experiences, failures, reflections, and successes, I will be able to impact your life in a positive way.

    The second reason I am putting this information together, printing it, and distributing one hundred copies at a cost to me is because I desire to make a difference. I do not have aspirations of being a writer, as you will soon conclude by the brevity of this book. I am a strong believer that the one thing that creates the vastest separation amongst men is quality information. I hope that you reading this book can find at least one thing to identify with and use the information to better your life.

Lastly, I believe that all relations should be symbiotic. I intend on giving a copy of this book to every one of my life insurance clients. Interestingly enough purchasing life insurance is already to the benefit of the client and I always do what is in the best interest of my clients, however I would like to bring more value to the client than the client brings to me.

Before we get started I want to thank and dedicate this writing to Diana Michel for standing by my side through the good and the bad. My daughters, for giving me a reason to push myself. My mother for not being very maternal and therefore causing me to be conditioned for life's challenges. My grandmother, for instilling old school Haitian principals in me. I didn't appreciate it at the time, but now I realize the importance of holding myself to my own personal standards. My father for being a fragmented presence in my life. Lastly, SUPER BIG SHOUTOUT to Theresa Jabbour, for literally coaching me and helping me work towards becoming my optimal self.

What Do You Think About You?

The most important thing that should matter to you is your opinion of yourself. I have one driving question; "am I the man I want to be?" If you can't be honest with yourself, odds are you aren't going to be honest with anyone else.

When I hold myself to a high standard of honesty, I don't do it for other people. I do it for myself. I do it so that I will follow through on my verbal commitments. Interestingly enough, that is all it takes to accomplish great things in life. You heard me right. First you say you are going to do something. Then you figure out how to do it. You work on it until it's done. That's it. Sure there will be obstacles, but if you really want something, you will overcome them.

Life Plan

You should have a grand plan for your life. You should decide what you want in terms of work, love, level of success, and quality of life. This plan should be selfish and not easily swayed by someone else. While working on this plan the right person will come and help you execute it, because it will be in alignment with their own plans.

I encourage you to break your plan down into 1, 3, 5, and 10 year increments. In addition, it isn't a plan if it isn't written down. Placing time frames will keep you on track and prevent you from having a decade or more zoom by absentmindedly. Think about it, all major corporations plan in 3, 5, and 10 year increments. Wouldn't it be wise for you to emulate their actions?

Guard Your Mind.

Everything that happens in your life is, in one way or another, a reflection of your previous thoughts. The way you think will determine how you handle obstacles, interact with people, view challenges, and ultimately your life. Your mind will either tell you that YOU CAN, or find every excuse for you not to do something.

Friends and family will more often than not be experts in why you should do something this way or that way despite not doing it themselves. People you know and love will, unknowingly to them, say things that lower your confidence and self worth. You have to forgive them and tune them out.

Speak to your subconscious mind. Silent or audibly if you must. Program it to make you strong, capable, positive, courageous, and relentless. Genetics and talent do play a part in some aspects of life, however the largest discriminator in life is mindset. Cultivate yours to give you the life you aspire for.

Eat Mental Wheaties

Speaking of cultivation. Read, listen to audiobooks, and engage in meaningful conversations that inspire mental growth. At the time of this writing it is 2016 and pretty much everyone has either a laptop, ipad, computer, or smartphone. Now ask yourself, how often does the manufacturer send an upgrade for that smart device? Yet millions of Americans simply do not read. They expect to progress in an ever changing world with the same software they had when they left high school or college.

We are in an ever evolving world economy where jobs are being phased out on a daily basis. If you are not keeping yourself informed and upgrading your skills, you may find yourself obsolete with a college degree and not getting paid what you are worth.

Focus

What are you focused on? What is your primary objective? I've never really had one until I turned thirty-one. A decade of my adult life, wasted! Not aimed at anything. It is very important to develop a vision for yourself and your life. More importantly, you have to focus on that vision daily. Prior to making decisions and taking actions ask yourself if what you're about to do, going to bring you closer or further away from that vision.

Everyone should have a plan for their lives. Unfortunately many people tie their plan to a specific job and when that doesn't workout, they quit on the plan and settle into something they can tolerate. There is more than one way to do most things in life. If you are FOCUSED and persistent you can do or have whatever it is you want.

The more focused you are, the faster things tend to happen.

Your Future is Greater Than Your Past.

I've done a lot of the things that I have wanted to do in my life. Ranging from being a combat veteran, riding motorcycles, earning a commercial pilot's license and getting a college degree. However, I do not spend much time elaborating on my past. Do you want to know why? Because, the best is yet to come.

Far too often people spend so much time reflecting and bragging about their glory days that they waste valuable time in the present and do nothing to maximize their future. THE BEST IS ALWAYS YET TO COME! I live by that mantra. Even as I write this. Is it another book? A movie? I don't know, but I know that I have more to offer than this one piece of work.

Don't become a middle aged man spending all of your time reminding people of how fast you were in high school. No one cares, and you can still do bigger and more significant things.

Be Great.

Why not desire to be great? Desire is the only thing that sets great people apart from average people? There are very few excuses for why a person can not be great especially in the most opportunity rich country in the world. People have overcome physical disabilities, poverty, and/or discrimination to make their mark on the world.

Greatness doesn't mean you have to be the world's greatest athlete or entertainer, it simply means that you are constantly striving to be a better you, and contributing to the best of your ability to society.

Having a positive impact on just one life may potentially alter the course of humanity.

Wishes or Goals?

Set goals and not wishes. More often than not people set wishes and call them goals. A goal has a time frame attached to it. In addition a goal is supported by actions that can be taken to help you achieve said goal.

Your goal may not seem realistic and that is okay. However the actions that you have outlined must be realistic. The more realistic your outline of actions are, the better your odds of achieving your goal. This topic is incredibly important. So important that I want to give you an example.

Let's pretend you work at a minimum wage job, and you want to go to Japan. You would first have to be honest with yourself and realize that you'll either need a raise or a job that earns more money. To obtain that job, you will most likely need more education or a new skill. Upon earning more money you would have to create a budget. Once you've figured your budget, the cost of the trip, and the amount of money you will need to pay your bills while you are not working; you'd have to attach a timeline to saving that money or find a way to make additional funds in order to expedite the process.

Hopefully my example discerns the difference between the goal stated in the last paragraph and simply saying I plan on traveling to Japan. The latter is simply a wish.

Unfortunately after failing to meet a handful or less of their "goals," most adults stop going after the things they want. Regardless of the goal, you have to be detailed. You must plan your work. Work your plan until you succeed or can no longer progress. If your progress is impeded, do not give up. Tweak the plan and work the modified version. Not having a plan is the equivalent of traveling in a foreign country without a map, GPS, or guide. Most importantly, if your goals aren't written down they do not exist. Look at them every morning and then again in the evening. Before going to sleep ask yourself if you've done ONE thing, today, required to reach your goal? Be accountable to yourself. Honor the words you speak to yourself.

At times it is better for you to focus on your trajectory than the end result. Too often people are so focused on the end result they never realize that they have veered off course.

Actions Not Results

I have failed a lot. In fact I would venture to say that I have failed a lot more than I've succeeded. Yet, I am living a more fulfilling life than most people. How can I be sure of that? Because I own my own time, which allows me to contribute to more causes and people than most people working 1 to 2 jobs are able to. I am able attend my children's events, see their milestones, and spend quality time with my family. All while earning a full-time income.

Nonetheless, the only thing that has gotten me through Army basic training, flight school, college, and many other challenges is the ability to keep the results in perspective. When I did well, I continued doing the things that worked. When I failed, I altered my approach, actions, habits, or sought additional help.

In all honesty, my first two years in insurance were terrible. But, I hung in there and hired a professional business coach. By using simple mindset changes, focus, and a few techniques I was able to change that in a relatively short period of time.

Don't let one, two, or a few failures keep you from achieving something that you really want. Unfortunately school fails children in this regard. If you fail a course or test as an adult, you can simply pay the price and retake it. Grade school simply doesn't follow a real world model, which conditions adults to believe that any ONE failure is a definitive representation of who they are as a person.

Health IS Wealth

Steve Jobs, the genius behind the iPhone was a billionaire and died prematurely of cancer. With that said, money can not buy health. Take care of your body. Educate yourself on the stuff that you are putting in your mouth. America has one of the, if not the highest, cancer rates in the world. I am not a genius, but I suspect it has something to do with what we are eating.

Wake up early and exercise. Stretch. Rest. Clear your mind. Take care of yourself. If you aren't feeling physically optimal, you are wasting brain power thinking about what is wrong with you. If you don't take the responsibility of taking care of your body, who will do it for you? Remember this one rule of thumb if nothing else: it's 80% diet, 20% exercise, and 100% your responsibility.

Lebron Has a Coach

People are often too caught up in their pride and end up with nothing, except for "PRIDE." Seek help when it is needed. Find an accountability partner, a mentor, and/or a vetted coach. There is nothing wrong with improving yourself and getting guidance from an outside reference.

The greatest basketball player in the NBA has coaches (more than one) and practices daily. Why then should you think you are above honing your craft and cultivating yourself? Improving yourself doesn't equate to being inadequate, it simply means that you can be better. Work towards being the best, and then work on beating yourself.

Everyone's An Expert

It seems like everywhere I turn, everyone's an expert on topics and fields they're barely qualified to speak about. I would suggest that you investigate issues for yourself. Do not simply shun the so-called experts. Listen to them, and then investigate what they tell you.

I've seen people miss out on great opportunities and lose money because of incorrect "expert" advice. When I speak of experts I want to also caution you about friends and family who specialize in the killing of dreams. They mean well, so don't hold it against them. Ensure that every decision you make is an informed one, which you've researched the ins and outs of on your own. .

Friend or Foe?

Influence is very subtle, however, it is highly powerful. Therefore you should always surround yourself with positive people of action. If you look at your circle of friends and they aren't aspiring to be more; you need a new circle of friends.

There is nothing wrong with having friends. In fact success for most people is based on their network. I encourage you to associate with people who are going places and help to push you forward, as opposed to negative influences that aim to hold you back.

Leave negative and/or comforting associations behind and put yourself in a group where you are the weakest link, and desire to become the strongest. Falling somewhere in the middle will drastically improve your quality of life.

The Right Partner

We are in a very sexually liberated period of human history and I wanted to make this section as unisexed as possible. If I fail to do that in any way, I hope that you will look past it and capture the idea being expressed. Too often people fall for the superficial aspects of an individual. Obviously it is only human nature, however you may be selling yourself short. I would advise that matters of the heart be approached from a more pragmatic standpoint.

Looks, sex appeal, and chemistry will probably fade with time. If you've chosen a partner solely based on sensational emotions, once the spark is gone, the relationship may quickly degrade from bliss to obligation.

I encourage you to find someone who has a life plan for themselves. Motivates you to be your best self and is dedicated to growth. I personally believe that I should be able to give what I am asking for, and that relationships aren't always 50/50. Some days your partner may have to come 90/10 for you and vice versa.

Projects Are for School

Giving your commitment to another human being or beings is an investment of your time. In my opinion, life is time. Thus, in essence you are investing your life.

Let's just imagine that the person you decided to put your life, time, effort, and energy into was a company? Would you invest in a company that is obviously going nowhere? Would you invest in a highly risky company? Do you think that you could, right now in this moment, take a company that is going under and turn it into a conglomerate? If not, then why would you believe that you can do that with a complicated free thinking human being?

Far too often I have seen people engage with someone who is chasing a low probability dream without a contingency plan, or simply stated, a loser. They believe they will get this person to make changes and yield a great return on their investment. I've yet to see someone succeed in turning a zero into a hero. If you know of such a person, inbox me.

Raising Adults

If you have children or one day intend on having children, here are a few things I think you should keep in mind. The words you speak to your children will either empower or cripple them. Choose your words wisely since you are creating their inner voice.

Do not rush them into the ways of the world, but bear in mind that the end product should be a strong, intelligent, capable adult. Are the things you're teaching them and the ways you're interacting with them, leading towards that goal?

Too often children are babied for too long, neglected, or left without cultivation. It is your job to educate your children. Not their teacher's. Their teacher is simply there to lay the foundation and create an employee.

Currently, many of the foundations being laid are faulty if not nonexistent. The real world does not give participation checks. Adults are left behind. And I have yet to hear of a business that gives a person extra time because they were not competent enough to complete their work in the allotted eight hours. Yet, these actions are being taken in schools all over America. Hmm..

Bad Parents

I am writing this book because I know what it is like to be raised without a good male role model. To be honest my mother wasn't so stellar either. Nonetheless I am grateful that neither of them abused me, and without their lack of parenting I would not be the person I am today.

I once read that our parents are the victims of victims. If you choose to believe that you will see that regardless of your circumstances with your parents, odds are, they didn't know any better.

I am not so audacious as to tell you how to interact with your parents. However I will say this, they're the only set you're going to get. Most likely you can't change them, however based on their toxicity you can choose to either accept them or distance yourself from them. I do request, regardless of how you choose to manage that relationship, you forgive them.

Respect

One of the army values that was instilled in me at the ripe age of eighteen was respect and I have kept their definition with me till today. That definition suggested that I treated others as they should be treated.

I interpreted that to mean that I offer my respect to everyone, until they fail to offer theirs in return. At which point I simply terminate interacting with them if possible.

Far too often, we fail to realize how offensive our speech, appearance, and mannerisms are. We are in a society, and should exhaust maximum effort to be as polite and courteous as possible. Anyone can be a jerk. Effort is rarely required to be subpar.

Together

There is a nevering ending effort to divide and conquer the entire planet. The monied and powerful unite for common interests, while keeping the rest of us divided. How might you ask?

The division is instilled mostly by competition and comparison, and it's instilled in us early. We end up cultivating a mindset that has us constantly evaluating ourselves, our possessions, and relationships with that of our peers. This focus on competition and comparison prevents us from being grateful for what we have. If you can not express and live in gratitude, you will live a life of struggle and strife.

Lastly this division keeps us from working together, slows progress, and is the primary reason the many are controlled by the few. Any great thing that has ever been built, has been built from collective effort.

Time

Time is not money. Time is by far more valuable than money. Money can be won, earned, lost, stolen, and then replaced; however once you lose a day it is gone forever.

The biggest problem most people suffer from is the idea that they can get to it in the future. There is, for the most part, only now.

I want to put that assumption to bed right now. Lets just assume you had 30,000 days to live. That would put your expiration date roughly a little over 82 years after your birth. Wake up call! By the time you are 30 years old you have already used approximately 10,900 of your 30,000 days assuming you'll live to see 82. Cut off another 5,000 days since I am pretty sure you wouldn't want to work from 70 to 82 and POOF; half of your life is gone before you know it.

If there is something you want to do, have, be, or see; I encourage you to get to work TODAY!

The relationship between time and money

Almost every person in the United States will spend the bulk of their adult life earning money. However very few of them will ever take the time to understand how money works. Yes, money can work and it can work for you.

The mass of Americans spend countless hours to research vacations, consumer goods, automobiles, concerts, and fashion; however when it is time to understand the contents of their retirement accounts, insurance policies, and other investments products they would prefer a cliffnote.

This social conditioning in regards to money in the United States is far more responsible for millions of people living in financial insecurity than any level of corporate greed, and it's probably by design. I would encourage you to make it your business to have a fair understanding of your money, retirement and investment products. Understanding the basics alone will change the trajectory of your life. The you of today IS responsible for the you of tomorrow.

Retirement

People start too late and invest too little. You have a higher statistical probability of living to an old age than you do of dying young. Unfortunately for far too many there isn't any gold in the golden years. Don't let this happen to you. It is far more important to start early than it is to start big.

When should you start saving? As soon as possible, however no later than the age of eighteen. Most people are unaware that you can open an Individual Retirement Account for their children under the age of 18. For context, $50 a month saved from age 15 to 65 earning a conservative average of 7% per year will grow to approximately $245,390. If you wait till you're 25 to start, that same $50 dollars will only yield you $120,530.

Hopefully this exemplifies the power of starting early when it comes to investing. Teach your children to start saving and investing young. If you don't know anything about investing, LEARN! If you're intent on not upgrading yourself, have your children speak to a retirement advisor at your bank.

Life Insurance

Like retiring, people purchase it too late and do not purchase enough. I encourage everyone to lock in their rate upon reaching the age of eighteen. Getting a policy this young will be more inexpensive than purchasing life insurance later on in life. Most importantly you are protecting your insurability, the ability to have life insurance coverage. Should you contract a disease, suffer a critical illness, become dependent on certain medications, etc.; you may become ineligible to purchase a policy in the future.

There are different types of policies, including some that invest your money or offer a return of your payments. Depending on your policy type and length of ownership you can access your money during emergencies without having to worry about a credit score or collateral.

In addition passing away is one of life's most predictable events and can be used to assist the next generation.

I am currently a life insurance broker in the state of Florida, Georgia, South Carolina, North Carolina, and Virginia (I will continue to add states as time moves forward). If you are looking for a quick and simplistic breakdown on the most popular types of life insurance, you can visit: wwwSummitInsuranceUSA.com

Rent

As you can see, I take time very seriously. With that said, think about the concept of paying rent. You spend most of your day working to pay for a place to live. Ironically when you are there, you are rarely ever living. You're simply recovering to go back to work. It gets worse. All of your timely monthly payments go to the owner. When you finally leave, you get a thank you in return. Your payments aren't even recorded on your credit report unless you use a service specifically tailored to do so.

I suggest that you cultivate a wealth building mindset and stay at your parent's house until you can buy. If that is not a possibility I suggest finding a friend who is looking to build equity as well, form a corporation, and buy a home as business associates.

How can you ever really do the things that you want; save and invest if you are giving the bulk of your income away month after month. Having a mortgage isn't ideal, however it is far better than paying over and over for something you will never own.

Home ownership (land ownership) is, in my experience, the foundation for building wealth and living a better life.

Less Stuff, More Life

Buying to keep up with the Jones more than anything else will ensure you never surpass them. Far too often people spend money they don't have on things they don't need. Why? To be cool? Let me tell you what is not cool. Being broke with the latest cellular device without any cellular service. Paying exaggerated prices to look like everyone else.

Despite having the latest and greatest of everything, if you are living paycheck to paycheck, you will always remain broke. Think about how often styles change, and the speed at which technology is upgraded. If you have the goal of remaining ahead of every trend, how can you ever have the resources for an emergency, retirement, new experiences, or travel?

Many people earn more than enough to have a great life, and yet don't. *Owning* a lot of stuff on credit is not success. Doing what you want is. Being faux rich, in my opinion, is slavery. Make sure you're pursuing accomplishments and not accumulation.

If your standard of living increases every time your income does, you will always remain in the same financial condition only with nicer things. Take for example, the countless NBA players that are broke within five years of "retiring" from the league.

Cars

Cars are not investments. NO ONE can predict the resale value of mass produced automobiles. How can anyone possibly predict the price of fuel, credit rates, or the likeliness of your vehicle being involved in an accident. All of these factors play a part in reselling your vehicle.

Buying a car that you can only drive to and from work is enslaving yourself. Considering in two to three years there will be a newer model and odds are some kid will hit yours with a shopping cart every time you go to Walmart. If you make under thirty thousand dollars a year, it is ridiculous to own a forty thousand dollar vehicle.

In addition, why would you incur more cost by adding aftermarket parts that simply add to the bill without adding to the value of the vehicle.

When I was in the Army, I always got a kick out of observing the privates with luxury cars that never left the barracks. The only place they ever drove to in style was work. At the end of the day, unless you are buying a very rare limited edition vehicle, you are buying a depreciating liability. Expensive cars quate to losing money while being exposed to constant risk.

Are You Costing You?

I want you to understand that everything has a cost. Laziness, procrastination, and especially a lack of willpower. Every book you put off is a guaranteed infliction on your future. Every discipline you neglect is a nail in a coffin containing your dreams. The cost of living a life on easy street is a life lived without fulfillment complimented with a greeters position at your local supermarket during your golden years. Technology and outsourcing is shrinking the labor force and enhancing the definition of entry level position. It is up to you to constantly add value to yourself and upgrade your skills. Capitalism aims to devalue you and your skills in order to increase profits. Governmental increases in minimum wage are always overdue. Pretending things will get better on their own only exacerbates problems. Always find a way to be and do more.

Leave Something Behind

How differently would your life have been if your grandfather left you something? Anything. A house, a car, money, land, or a family business? Take a moment and think about it. Now ask yourself, how differently things would have been if your father passed on any of those things?

Unfortunately, you don't have any control over that. However, you do have control over what you can leave behind. Your descendants are your legacy, and as you work and design your life, you should keep them in mind. This will assist you in making better long term decisions.

When it is all said and done, the only people who will sincerely carry your torch are your progeny. If you'd like to live a life with meaning, to live your life not only for yourself, but for future generations as well.

I leave you with this question. What will your life have meant when you come to the end? Fortunately, you get to answer this question now and make your answers become your reality. Your life is your own masterpiece to design. Do not allow the constrictions of society keep you from living it your way.

Closing Thoughts.

This book does not have the power to change your life.
You are the only person that can change your life. Ultimately,
your ability **to be honest with yourself, and hold yourself
accountable** is the deciding factor. I simply hope I've given
you a few short cuts.. Take everything with a grain of salt as
life is in constant flux, and live your life by your own
philosophies.

All change starts from within. You don't have much control
over the actions of others or society's perceptions. Thus, you
have to be the best you that you can be. You must work on
yourself daily. If you work hard on your mental game, you
will take the actions to get you to where you intend on going.
But only you can work on you, and you have to do it for you!
I wrote this hoping to share some of the mindsets that I've
cultivated after much failure, pain, and struggle. If you get
nothing else from this book, I want you to adopt and use this
next statement as fuel to drive you.

"No one is coming to help you. You better figure it out." In
all honesty there is help out there, but you have to go find it.
Have the mindset that only you can help you, and force
yourself to take action. Nothing is going to trump taking
action, hard work, consistency, and tenacity. Do not waste
your time in hope.

Contact Steve Isidor

Website: SteveIsidor.com
Instagram: UrInsuranceAgent
Follow the hashtag #DownToEarthMotivation on IG
Twitter: UrInsAgent
Facebook: /steve.isidor